Contents

Folder Centers

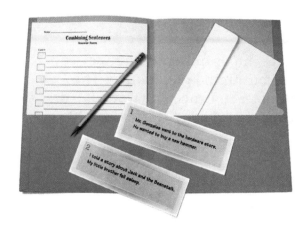

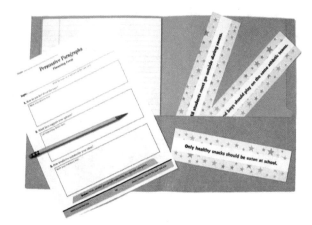

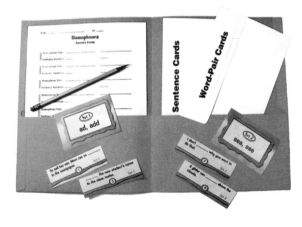

Language Arts Centers
Take It to Your Seat

What's Great About This Book

Centers are a wonderful way for students to practice important skills, but they can take up a lot of classroom space and require time-consuming preparation. The 18 centers in this book are self-contained and portable. Students may work at a desk or even on the floor using a lapboard for writing. Once you've made the centers, they're ready to use any time.

Everything You Need

- Teacher direction page
    How to make the center
    Description of student task
- Full-color materials needed for the center
- Reproducible answer forms with student directions
- Answer key

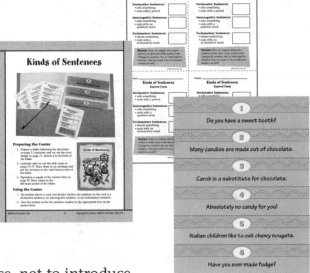

Using the Centers

The centers are intended for skill practice, not to introduce skills. It is important to model the use of each center before students do the task independently.

Considering these questions in advance will avoid later confusion:

- Will students select a center or will you assign the centers?
- Will there be a specific block of time for centers or will the centers be used throughout the day?
- Where will you place the centers for easy access by students?
- What procedure will students use when they need help with the center tasks?
- Where will students put completed work?
- How will you track the tasks and centers completed by each student?

Making a Folder Center

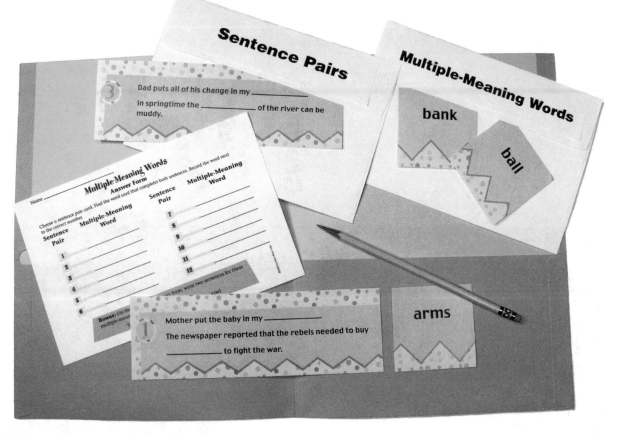

Folder centers are easily stored in a box or file crate. Students take a folder to their desks to complete the task.

Materials

- folder with pockets
- envelope(s)
- marking pens
- glue

Steps to Follow

1. Laminate and cut out the cover design. Glue it to the front of the folder.

2. Place answer forms, writing paper, and any other supplies in the left-hand pocket.

3. Place each set of task cards in an envelope in the right-hand pocket.

Antonyms

Preparing the Center

1. Prepare a folder following the directions on page 3. Laminate and cut out the cover design on page 7. Attach it to the front of the folder.

2. Laminate and cut out the task cards on pages 9—15. Place each set in an envelope, mark the set color on the envelope, and put the envelopes in the right-hand pocket of the folder. (Page 6 provides blank cards. Add words of your own or develop additional tasks.)

3. Reproduce a supply of the answer form on page 5 and blank task cards on page 6. Place copies in the left-hand pocket of the folder.

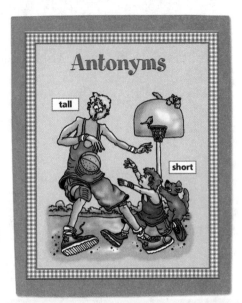

Using the Center

1. The student matches the task cards to create antonym pairs.

2. Then the student writes the color of the card set on the answer form and records the antonyms.

Name _____

Card Set Color _____

Antonyms
Answer Form

Choose an envelope. Write the color of the card set on this form. Match the cards to create antonym pairs. Record the antonym pairs below.

1. _____
   _____

2. _____
   _____

3. _____
   _____

4. _____
   _____

5. _____
   _____

6. _____
   _____

7. _____
   _____

8. _____
   _____

9. _____
   _____

Bonus: Create new task cards by filling in blank task cards with five new antonym pairs.

Name _____

Card Set Color _____

Antonyms
Answer Form

Choose an envelope. Write the color of the card set on this form. Match the cards to create antonym pairs. Record the antonym pairs below.

1. _____
   _____

2. _____
   _____

3. _____
   _____

4. _____
   _____

5. _____
   _____

6. _____
   _____

7. _____
   _____

8. _____
   _____

9. _____
   _____

Bonus: Create new task cards by filling in blank task cards with five new antonym pairs.

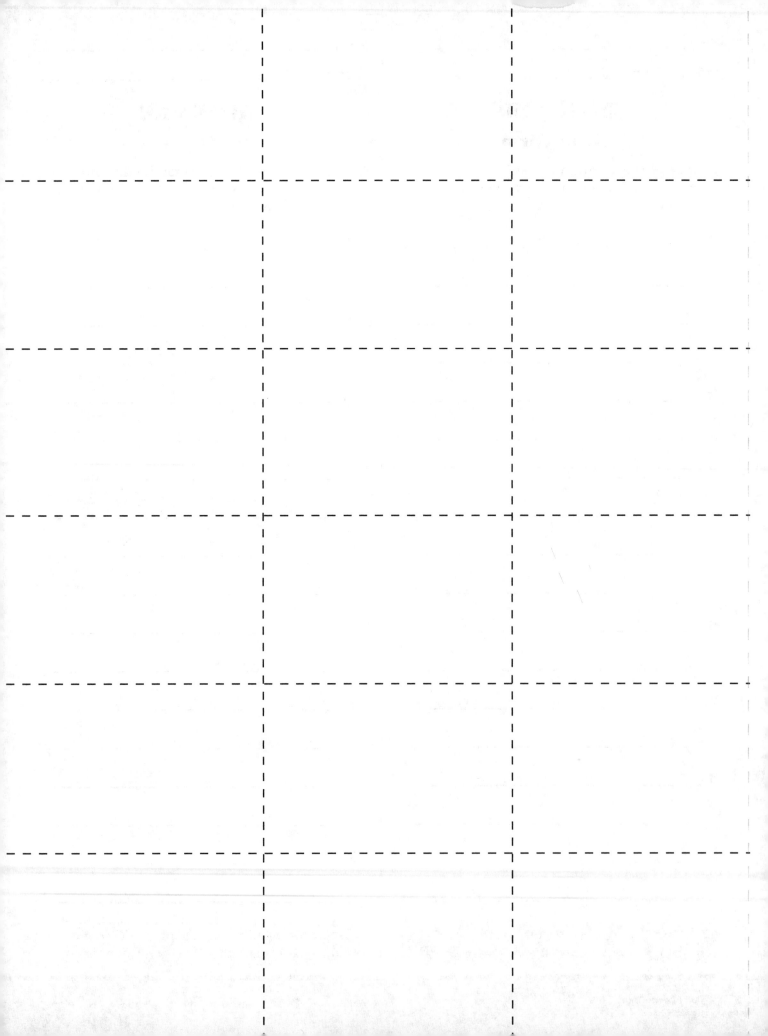

Antonyms

tall

short

absent	achieve	advance
affirm	admire	attack
awkward	annoy	bent
present	fail	retreat
deny	detest	defend
graceful	soothe	straight

Antonyms

Antonyms

Antonyms

Antonyms

Antonyms

Antonyms

Antonyms

Antonyms

Antonyms

Antonyms

Antonyms

Antonyms

Antonyms

Antonyms

Antonyms

Antonyms

Antonyms

Antonyms

brave	blunt	capture
cheap	cruel	destroy
expand	forgive	fresh
cowardly	sharp	release
expensive	kind	create
shrink	blame	stale

Antonyms

Antonyms

Antonyms

Antonyms

Antonyms

Antonyms

Antonyms

Antonyms

Antonyms

Antonyms

Antonyms

Antonyms

Antonyms

Antonyms

Antonyms

Antonyms

Antonyms

Antonyms

idle	innocent	level
obvious	plentiful	positive
praise	prohibit	ridiculous
active	guilty	uneven
hidden	sparse	negative
criticism	allow	sensible

Antonyms

Antonyms

Antonyms

Antonyms

Antonyms

Antonyms

Antonyms

Antonyms

Antonyms

Antonyms

Antonyms

Antonyms

Antonyms

Antonyms

Antonyms

Antonyms

Antonyms

Antonyms

sharp	thorough	unique
vanish	rapid	stiff
suspect	temporary	triumph
dull	incomplete	common
appear	slow	flexible
trust	permanent	defeat

Antonyms

Antonyms

Antonyms

Antonyms

Antonyms

Antonyms

Antonyms

Antonyms

Antonyms

Antonyms

Antonyms

Antonyms

Antonyms

Antonyms

Antonyms

Antonyms

Antonyms

Antonyms

Alphabetical Order

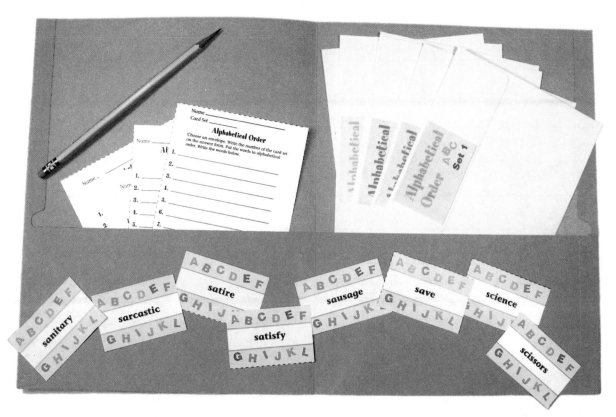

Preparing the Center

1. Prepare a folder following the directions on page 3. Laminate and cut out the cover design on page 19. Attach it to the front of the folder.

2. Laminate and cut out the task cards on pages 21–25. Place each set in an envelope, label the envelope with the set number, and put the envelopes in the right-hand pocket of the folder.

3. Reproduce a supply of the answer form on page 18. Place copies in the left-hand pocket of the folder.

Using the Center

1. The student selects an envelope and puts the words inside in alphabetical order. (The task becomes more difficult with each succeeding envelope.)

2. The student writes the number of the card set on the answer form, and then writes the words in order.

Name _____

Card Set _____

Alphabetical Order

Choose an envelope. Write the number of the card set on the answer form. Put the words in alphabetical order. Write the words below.

1. _____

2. _____

3. _____

4. _____

5. _____

6. _____

7. _____

8. _____

Bonus: Write sentences using the words. The sentences should show that you understand the meaning of each word.

©2002 by Evan-Moor Corp.

Name _____

Card Set _____

Alphabetical Order

Choose an envelope. Write the number of the card set on the answer form. Put the words in alphabetical order. Write the words below.

1. _____

2. _____

3. _____

4. _____

5. _____

6. _____

7. _____

8. _____

Bonus: Write sentences using the words. The sentences should show that you understand the meaning of each word.

©2002 by Evan-Moor Corp.

Name _____

Card Set _____

Alphabetical Order

Choose an envelope. Write the number of the card set on the answer form. Put the words in alphabetical order. Write the words below.

1. _____

2. _____

3. _____

4. _____

5. _____

6. _____

7. _____

8. _____

Bonus: Write sentences using the words. The sentences should show that you understand the meaning of each word.

©2002 by Evan-Moor Corp.

Name _____

Card Set _____

Alphabetical Order

Choose an envelope. Write the number of the card set on the answer form. Put the words in alphabetical order. Write the words below.

1. _____

2. _____

3. _____

4. _____

5. _____

6. _____

7. _____

8. _____

Bonus: Write sentences using the words. The sentences should show that you understand the meaning of each word.

©2002 by Evan-Moor Corp.

Alphabetical Order

A B C D E F   A B C D E F

acid   **chase**

G H I J K L   G H I J K L

A B C D E F   A B C D E F   A B C D E F

environment   **fiction**   **machine**

G H I J K L   G H I J K L   G H I J K L

A B C D E F   A B C D E F   A B C D E F

omnivorous   **revise**   **speculate**

G H I J K L   G H I J K L   G H I J K L

A B C D E F   A B C D E F

mortar   **morning**

G H I J K L   G H I J K L

A B C D E F   A B C D E F   A B C D E F

owner   **package**   **plaster**

G H I J K L   G H I J K L   G H I J K L

A B C D E F   A B C D E F   A B C D E F

quote   **racket**   **reason**

G H I J K L   G H I J K L   G H I J K L

Alphabetical Order

A B C D E

Alphabetical Order

A B C D E

Alphabetical Order

A B C D E

Alphabetical Order

A B C D E

Alphabetical Order

A B C D E

Alphabetical Order

A B C D E

Alphabetical Order

A B C D E

Alphabetical Order

A B C D E

Alphabetical Order

A B C D E

Alphabetical Order

A B C D E

Alphabetical Order

A B C D E

Alphabetical Order

A B C D E

Alphabetical Order

A B C D E

Alphabetical Order

A B C D E

Alphabetical Order

A B C D E

Alphabetical Order

A B C D E

Alphabetical Order

A B C D E

Alphabetical Order

A B C D E

Alphabetical Order ABC

Set 3

sarcastic	sanitary

satire	satisfy	save

sausage	scissors	science

Alphabetical Order ABC

Set 4

grief	grind

groom	grouch	ground

group	grove	groggy

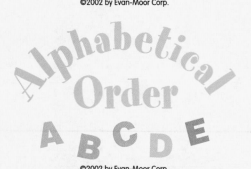

Alphabetical Order ABC

Set 5

A B C D E F | A B C D E F

hyacinth | **hydraulic**

G H I J K L | G H I J K L

A B C D E F | A B C D E F | A B C D E F

hydrogen | **hyena** | **hygiene**

G H I J K L | G H I J K L | G H I J K L

A B C D E F | A B C D E F | A B C D E F

hyperactive | **hypnotic** | **hypothesis**

G H I J K L | G H I J K L | G H I J K L

Alphabetical Order ABC

Set 6

A B C D E F | A B C D E F

radar | **radial**

G H I J K L | G H I J K L

A B C D E F | A B C D E F | A B C D E F

radiant | **radiate** | **radiator**

G H I J K L | G H I J K L | G H I J K L

A B C D E F | A B C D E F | A B C D E F

radical | **radio** | **radioactive**

G H I J K L | G H I J K L | G H I J K L

Alphabetical Order

A B C D E

©2002 by Evan-Moor Corp.

Alphabetical Order

A B C D E

©2002 by Evan-Moor Corp.

Alphabetical Order

A B C D E

©2002 by Evan-Moor Corp.

Alphabetical Order

A B C D E

©2002 by Evan-Moor Corp.

Alphabetical Order

A B C D E

©2002 by Evan-Moor Corp.

Alphabetical Order

A B C D E

©2002 by Evan-Moor Corp.

Alphabetical Order

A B C D E

©2002 by Evan-Moor Corp.

Alphabetical Order

A B C D E

©2002 by Evan-Moor Corp.

Alphabetical Order

A B C D E

©2002 by Evan-Moor Corp.

Alphabetical Order

A B C D E

©2002 by Evan-Moor Corp.

Alphabetical Order

A B C D E

©2002 by Evan-Moor Corp.

Alphabetical Order

A B C D E

©2002 by Evan-Moor Corp.

Alphabetical Order

A B C D E

©2002 by Evan-Moor Corp.

Alphabetical Order

A B C D E

©2002 by Evan-Moor Corp.

Alphabetical Order

A B C D E

©2002 by Evan-Moor Corp.

Alphabetical Order

A B C D E

©2002 by Evan-Moor Corp.

Alphabetical Order

A B C D E

©2002 by Evan-Moor Corp.

Alphabetical Order

A B C D E

©2002 by Evan-Moor Corp.

Parts of Speech

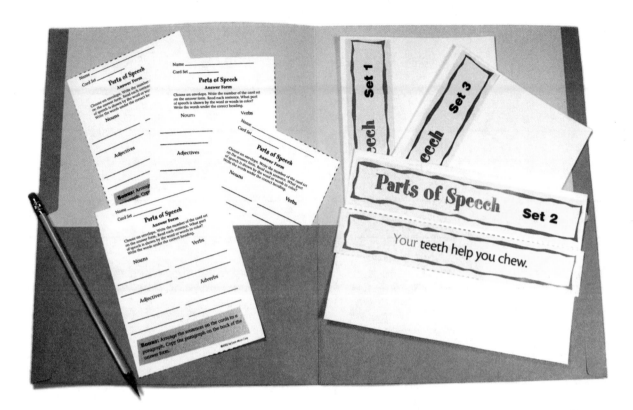

Preparing the Center

1. Prepare a folder following the directions on page 3. Laminate and cut out the cover design on page 29. Attach it to the front of the folder.

2. Laminate and cut out the task cards on pages 31–35. Place each set in an envelope, label the envelope with the number of the set, and put the envelopes in the right-hand pocket of the folder.

3. Reproduce a supply of the answer form on page 28. Place copies in the left-hand pocket of the folder.

Using the Center

1. The student chooses a task card, reads the sentence, and decides what part of speech is represented by the word in color.

2. The student writes the word on the answer form in the appropriate column.

Name _____

Card Set _____

Parts of Speech
Answer Form

Choose an envelope. Write the number of the card set on the answer form. Read each sentence. What part of speech is shown by the word or words in color? Write the words under the correct heading.

Nouns	Verbs
_____	_____
_____	_____

Adjectives	Adverbs
_____	_____
_____	_____

Bonus: Arrange the sentences on the cards in a paragraph. Copy the paragraph on the back of the answer form.

Name _____

Card Set _____

Parts of Speech
Answer Form

Choose an envelope. Write the number of the card set on the answer form. Read each sentence. What part of speech is shown by the word or words in color? Write the words under the correct heading.

Nouns	Verbs
_____	_____
_____	_____

Adjectives	Adverbs
_____	_____
_____	_____

Bonus: Arrange the sentences on the cards in a paragraph. Copy the paragraph on the back of the answer form.

Name _____

Card Set _____

Parts of Speech
Answer Form

Choose an envelope. Write the number of the card set on the answer form. Read each sentence. What part of speech is shown by the word or words in color? Write the words under the correct heading.

Nouns	Verbs
_____	_____
_____	_____

Adjectives	Adverbs
_____	_____
_____	_____

Bonus: Arrange the sentences on the cards in a paragraph. Copy the paragraph on the back of the answer form.

Name _____

Card Set _____

Parts of Speech
Answer Form

Choose an envelope. Write the number of the card set on the answer form. Read each sentence. What part of speech is shown by the word or words in color? Write the words under the correct heading.

Nouns	Verbs
_____	_____
_____	_____

Adjectives	Adverbs
_____	_____
_____	_____

Bonus: Arrange the sentences on the cards in a paragraph. Copy the paragraph on the back of the answer form.

Parts of Speech

Parts of Speech

Animals sleep in many different places.

Horses and giraffes sleep standing up.

Hippos sleep in a big heap.

Bats sleep upside down.

I sleep in a comfortable, warm bed.

Birds perch on a branch as they sleep.

Parts of Speech

Parts of Speech

Parts of Speech

Parts of Speech

Parts of Speech

Parts of Speech

Parts of Speech

Parts of Speech

Your teeth help you chew.

They break food into small pieces.

Teeth help you talk too.

Teeth support muscles around the mouth.

They give your face shape.

Your teeth have three important jobs.

Parts of Speech

Parts of Speech

Parts of Speech

Parts of Speech

Parts of Speech

Parts of Speech

Parts of Speech

Parts of Speech

Set 3

Some seeds move on the wind.

Some seeds have wing-like parts.

Other seeds have hooks or stickers.

Some seeds float on water to new places.

People plant seeds in their gardens.

Seeds travel in many different ways.

Parts of Speech

Parts of Speech

Parts of Speech

Parts of Speech

Parts of Speech

Parts of Speech

Parts of Speech

Synonyms

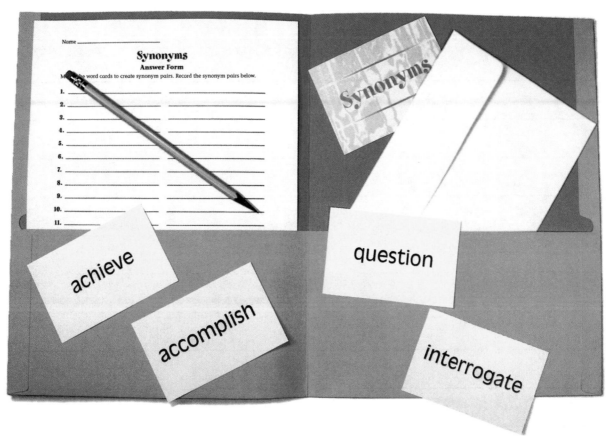

Preparing the Center

1. Prepare a folder following the directions on page 3. Laminate and cut out the cover design on page 39. Attach it to the front of the folder.

2. Laminate and cut out the task cards on pages 41–47. Place them in an envelope and put the envelope in the right-hand pocket of the folder.

3. Reproduce a supply of the answer form on page 38. Place copies in the left-hand pocket of the folder.

4. Add several blank index cards to the left-hand pocket.

Using the Center

1. The student matches the task cards to create synonym pairs.

2. Then the student records the synonyms on the answer form.

Synonyms
Answer Form

Match the word cards to create synonym pairs. Record the synonym pairs below.

1. _____   _____

2. _____   _____

3. _____   _____

4. _____   _____

5. _____   _____

6. _____   _____

7. _____   _____

8. _____   _____

9. _____   _____

10. _____   _____

11. _____   _____

12. _____   _____

13. _____   _____

14. _____   _____

15. _____   _____

16. _____   _____

Bonus: Create new task cards by writing new synonym pairs on index cards. Write one word on each side of the card and cut the card in half.

Synonyms

capable	competent
achieve	accomplish
question	interrogate
astonish	surprise

Synonyms

Synonyms

Synonyms

Synonyms

Synonyms

Synonyms

Synonyms

Synonyms

start	initiate
border	edge
brave	courageous
calm	serene

Synonyms

Synonyms

Synonyms

Synonyms

Synonyms

Synonyms

Synonyms

Synonyms

decrease	lessen
danger	peril
disaster	catastrophe
finish	complete

Synonyms

Synonyms

Synonyms

Synonyms

Synonyms

Synonyms

Synonyms

Synonyms

own	possess
beginner	novice
praise	applaud
supply	furnish

Synonyms

Synonyms

Synonyms

Synonyms

Synonyms

Synonyms

Synonyms

Synonyms

Combining Sentences

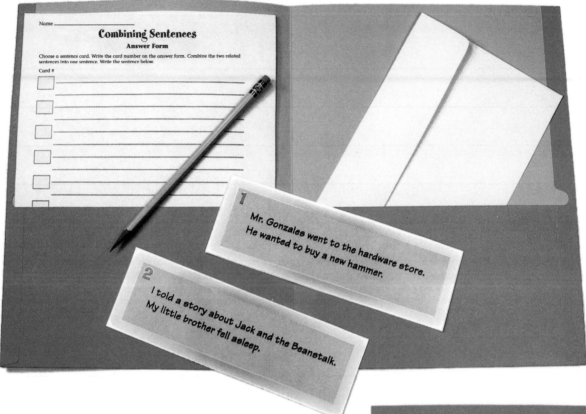

Preparing the Center

1. Prepare a folder following the directions on page 3. Laminate and cut out the cover design on page 51. Attach it to the front of the folder.

2. Laminate and cut out the task cards on pages 53–57. Place them in an envelope and put the envelope in the right-hand pocket of the folder.

3. Reproduce a supply of the answer form on page 50. Place copies in the left-hand pocket of the folder.

Using the Center

1. The student chooses a task card and reads the two related sentences on the card.

2. Then the student combines the sentences into a single sentence and writes the sentence on the answer form.

Name _____

Combining Sentences

Answer Form

Choose a sentence card. Write the card number on the answer form. Combine the two related sentences into one sentence. Write the sentence below.

Card #

☐ _____

_____

☐ _____

_____

☐ _____

_____

☐ _____

_____

☐ _____

_____

☐ _____

_____

Bonus: Label each sentence combination telling how you combined the sentences.

• Introductory Phrase—IP
   If you turned one sentence into a phrase and placed it at the beginning of the new sentence.

• Modifying Phrase—MP
   If you included the information in one sentence as a modifying phrase after the subject.

• Compound Sentence—CS
   If you combined the two sentences by using a connecting word such as *and, to, but, since,* or *because.*

Combining Sentences

1

Mr. Gonzales went to the hardware store.
He wanted to buy a new hammer.

2

I told a story about Jack and the Beanstalk.
My little brother fell asleep.

3

Hannah fell down.
She learned that rollerblading can be dangerous.

4

Kanisha found a book for her report.
She used the library browser on the computer.

Combining Sentences

Combining Sentences

Combining Sentences

Combining Sentences

5

Gramps is my dog.
He loves to jump over the fence.

6

Mrs. Francis is the school nurse.
She keeps my cough medicine in her office.

7

Peter, Frank, and Cisco are my friends.
We like to play soccer.

8

Lynette is my neighbor.
She has a beautiful rose garden.

Combining Sentences

Combining Sentences

Combining Sentences

Combining Sentences

9

Steve and Josh went to the beach.
They wanted to explore the tide pools.

10

Andi learned to do a back flip.
She learned to do a cartwheel too.

11

Josefina is our new student body president.
She got the most votes in the runoff election.

12

The mail carrier brought a big envelope.
It's my mother's birthday today.

Combining Sentences

Combining Sentences

Combining Sentences

Combining Sentences

Analogies

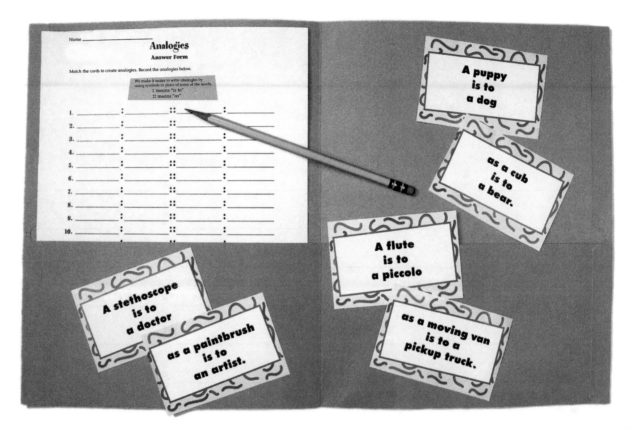

Preparing the Center

1. Prepare a folder following the directions on page 3. Laminate and cut out the cover design on page 61. Attach it to the front of the folder.

2. Laminate and cut out the task cards on pages 63–67. Place them in an envelope and put the envelope in the right-hand pocket of the folder.

3. Reproduce a supply of the answer form on page 60. Place copies in the left-hand pocket of the folder.

Using the Center

1. The student matches the task cards to create analogies.

2. Then the student records the analogies on the answer form.

Analogies

Answer Form

Match the cards to create analogies. Record the analogies below.

> We make it easier to write analogies by
> using symbols in place of some of the words.
> **:** means "is to"
> **::** means "as"

1. _____ : _____ :: _____ : _____
2. _____ : _____ :: _____ : _____
3. _____ : _____ :: _____ : _____
4. _____ : _____ :: _____ : _____
5. _____ : _____ :: _____ : _____
6. _____ : _____ :: _____ : _____
7. _____ : _____ :: _____ : _____
8. _____ : _____ :: _____ : _____
9. _____ : _____ :: _____ : _____
10. _____ : _____ :: _____ : _____
11. _____ : _____ :: _____ : _____
12. _____ : _____ :: _____ : _____

Bonus: Write and illustrate a new analogy on the back of the answer form.

Analogies

Gloves are to hands as

shoes are to feet

A stethoscope is to a doctor

as a paintbrush is to an artist.

A tablecloth is to a table

as a scarf is to a head.

Heavy is to light

as speedy is to pokey.

A puppy is to a dog

as a cub is to a bear.

Analogies

Analogies

Analogies

Analogies

Analogies

Analogies

Analogies

Analogies

Film is to a camera

as ink is to a pen.

A hamster is to a running wheel

as a runner is to a track.

Gas is to tank

as salt is to shaker.

Suspenders are to pants

as trellises are to vines.

Analogies

Analogies

Analogies

Analogies

Analogies

Analogies

Analogies

Analogies

**Model T
is to
automobile**

**as Pony Express
is to
mail service.**

**A flute
is to
a piccolo**

**as a moving van
is to
a pickup truck.**

**Three
is to
nine**

**as ten
is to
one hundred.**

**Fast
is to
rapid**

**as still
is to
calm.**

Analogies

Analogies

Analogies

Analogies

Analogies

Analogies

Analogies

Analogies

Kinds of Sentences

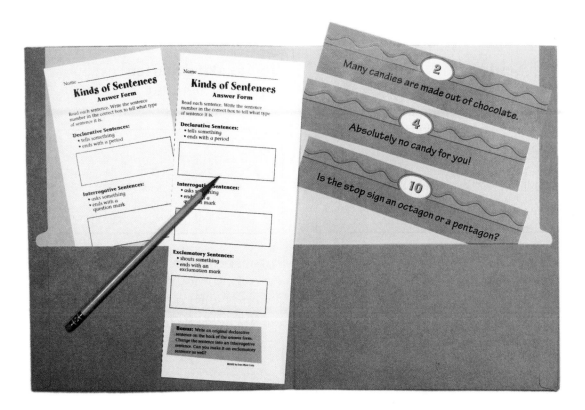

Preparing the Center

1. Prepare a folder following the directions on page 3. Laminate and cut out the cover design on page 71. Attach it to the front of the folder.

2. Laminate and cut out the task cards on pages 73–77. Place them in an envelope and put the envelope in the right-hand pocket of the folder.

3. Reproduce a supply of the answer form on page 70. Place copies in the left-hand pocket of the folder.

Using the Center

1. The student selects a card and decides whether the sentence on the card is a declarative sentence, an interrogative sentence, or an exclamatory sentence.

2. Then the student writes the sentence number in the appropriate box on the answer form.

Name _____

Kinds of Sentences
Answer Form

Read each sentence. Write the sentence number in the correct box to tell what type of sentence it is.

Declarative Sentences:
- tells something
- ends with a period

Interrogative Sentences:
- asks something
- ends with a question mark

Exclamatory Sentences:
- shouts something
- ends with an exclamation mark

Bonus: Write an original declarative sentence on the back of the answer form. Change the sentence into an interrogative sentence. Can you make it an exclamatory sentence as well?

Name _____

Kinds of Sentences
Answer Form

Read each sentence. Write the sentence number in the correct box to tell what type of sentence it is.

Declarative Sentences:
- tells something
- ends with a period

Interrogative Sentences:
- asks something
- ends with a question mark

Exclamatory Sentences:
- shouts something
- ends with an exclamation mark

Bonus: Write an original declarative sentence on the back of the answer form. Change the sentence into an interrogative sentence. Can you make it an exclamatory sentence as well?

©2002 by Evan-Moor Corp.

Kinds of Sentences

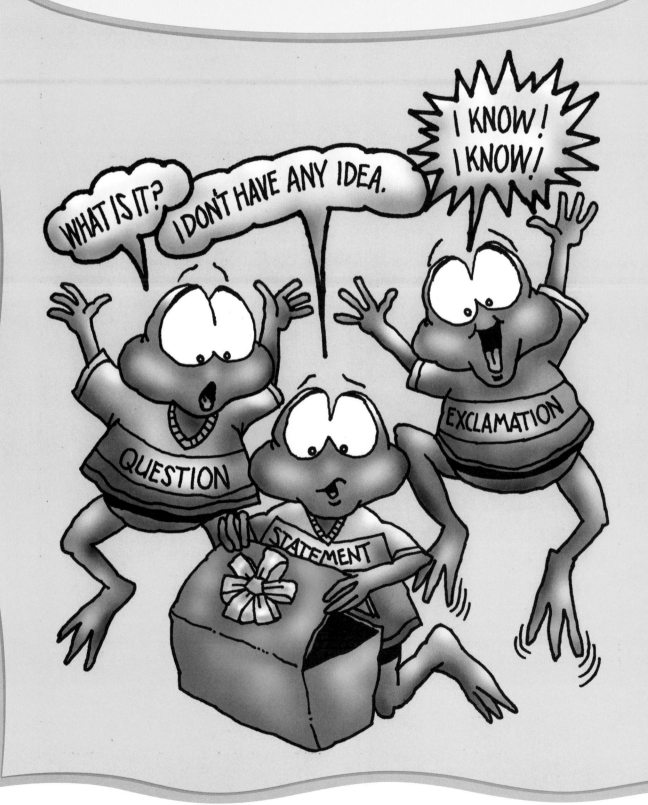

1

Do you have a sweet tooth

2

Many candies are made out of chocolate

3

Carob is a substitute for chocolate

4

Absolutely no candy for you

5

Italian children like to eat chewy nougats

6

Have you ever made fudge

Kinds of Sentences

Kinds of Sentences

Kinds of Sentences

Kinds of Sentences

Kinds of Sentences

Kinds of Sentences

7

Add two numbers to get a sum

8

Mathematics is the science of numbers

9

I love all kinds of math

10

Is the stop sign an octagon or a pentagon

11

You divide to find the quotient

12

I can't believe I got the answer

Kinds of Sentences

Kinds of Sentences

Kinds of Sentences

Kinds of Sentences

Kinds of Sentences

Kinds of Sentences

13

Help, I'm losing my grip

14

Rock climbing is a strenuous sport

15

Can you rappel down the side of a mountain

16

When the guide yells, "Belay!" I respond, "Belay on"

17

Hiking is not the same as rock climbing

18

Do you have climbing shoes

Kinds of Sentences

Kinds of Sentences

Kinds of Sentences

Kinds of Sentences

Kinds of Sentences

Kinds of Sentences

Main Ideas & Supporting Details

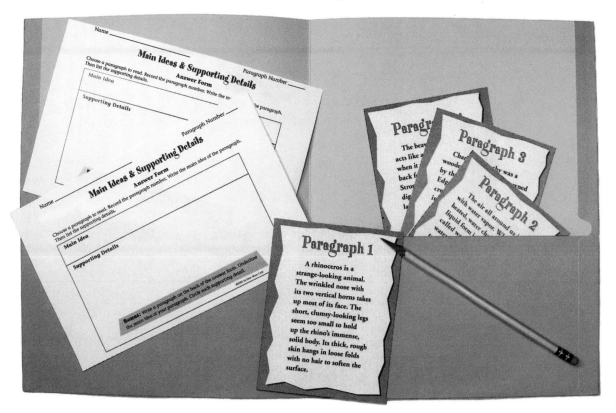

Preparing the Center

1. Prepare a folder following the directions on page 3. Laminate and cut out the cover design on page 81. Attach it to the front of the folder.

2. Laminate and cut out the task cards on pages 83 and 85. Place them in an envelope and put the envelope in the right-hand pocket of the folder.

3. Reproduce a supply of the answer form on page 80. Place copies in the left-hand pocket of the folder.

Using the Center

1. The student chooses a task card and reads the paragraph on the card.

2. Then the student writes the main idea of the paragraph on the answer form and lists the supporting details.

Name _____ Paragraph Number _____

Main Ideas & Supporting Details
Answer Form

Choose a paragraph to read. Record the paragraph number. Write the main idea of the paragraph. Then list the supporting details.

Main Idea

Supporting Details

Bonus: Write a paragraph on the back of the answer form. Underline the main idea of your paragraph. Circle each supporting detail.

©2002 by Evan-Moor Corp.

- -

Name _____ Paragraph Number _____

Main Ideas & Supporting Details
Answer Form

Choose a paragraph to read. Record the paragraph number. Write the main idea of the paragraph. Then list the supporting details.

Main Idea

Supporting Details

Bonus: Write a paragraph on the back of the answer form. Underline the main idea of your paragraph. Circle each supporting detail.

©2002 by Evan-Moor Corp.

Main Ideas

Supporting Details

Paragraph 1

A rhinoceros is a strange-looking animal. The wrinkled nose with its two vertical horns takes up most of its face. The short, clumsy-looking legs seem too small to hold up the rhino's immense, solid body. Its thick, rough skin hangs in loose folds with no hair to soften the surface.

Paragraph 2

The air all around us is filled with water vapor. When it is heated, water changes from a liquid form into an invisible gas called water vapor. When the water vapor in the air cools, it turns back into tiny droplets of water to form a cloud. The same water moves from liquid form to water vapor and back to liquid form over and over again. This pattern of change is called the water cycle.

Paragraph 3

Charlie McCarthy was a wooden dummy. He was owned by the famous ventriloquist, Edgar Bergen. Mr. Bergen created Charlie while he was in high school. Charlie traveled around the world with Mr. Bergen. They performed for many people. Charlie was so popular that he got more mail than Mr. Bergen did. Even a puppet can be a famous star.

Paragraph 4

The beaver's broad tail acts like a rudder to steer when it swims. Its webbed back feet help it swim. Strong front paws help it dig and carry. Two very large orange front teeth gnaw down trees. All in all, the beaver is perfectly equipped to be a pond engineer.

Main Ideas
&
Supporting Details

Main Ideas
&
Supporting Details

Main Ideas
&
Supporting Details

Main Ideas
&
Supporting Details

Paragraph 5

Most people remember George Washington as an important American statesman, the first U.S. president. He was also important to the development of modern farming. At his farm in Virginia, he studied the best way to plant and harvest crops. He experimented with new farming equipment. He even built a special 16-sided barn for threshing the wheat that he grew. He kept meticulous records about each crop and its yield.

Paragraph 6

The Nile is one of the birthplaces of modern civilization. It is the longest river in the world. The name *Nile* came from the Greek word *neilos*, which means "valley." Water from the river and the fertile soil along its banks made this river valley a good place for ancient peoples to live and farm.

Paragraph 7

Did you know that whales can be identified by the shape and size of their blows? The blue whale's blow is narrow and high. Right whales make two low blows with their twin blowholes. The humpback whale has a low blow. The sperm whale makes a blow that is angled forward and to the left. It's important to know your blows.

Paragraph 8

Kenya's flag has three stripes with a Masai warrior's shield in its center. This simple design has important significance for the Kenyan people. The black on the flag represents the people. The red stands for the blood shed in Kenya's fight for independence. The green represents the fertility of the land. The white represents peace. The shield in the center represents Kenya's pride and tradition.

Main Ideas

&

Supporting Details

Main Ideas

&

Supporting Details

Main Ideas

&

Supporting Details

Main Ideas

&

Supporting Details

Metaphors & Similes

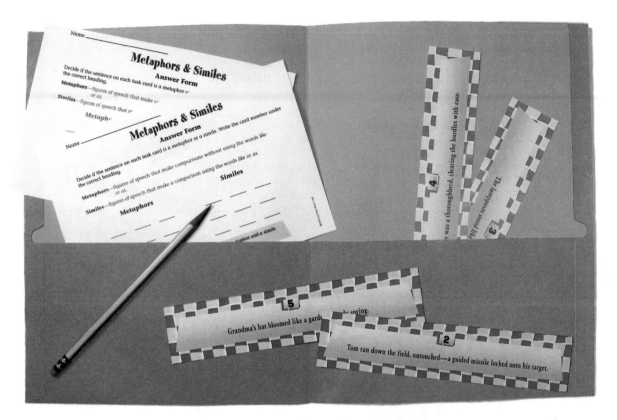

Preparing the Center

1. Prepare a folder following the directions on page 3. Laminate and cut out the cover design on page 89. Attach it to the front of the folder.

2. Laminate and cut out the task cards on pages 91 and 93. Place them in an envelope and put the envelope in the right-hand pocket of the folder.

3. Reproduce a supply of the answer form on page 88. Place copies in the left-hand pocket of the folder.

Using the Center

1. The student classifies comparisons on the task cards as metaphors or similes.

2. Then the student records the number of each task card in the appropriate column on the answer form.

Metaphors & Similes

Answer Form

Decide if the sentence on each task card is a metaphor or a simile. Write the card number under the correct heading.

Metaphors—figures of speech that make comparisons without using the words *like* or *as.*

Similes—figures of speech that make a comparison using the words *like* or *as.*

Metaphors   Similes

_____ _____ _____   _____ _____ _____

_____ _____ _____   _____ _____ _____

_____ _____ _____   _____ _____ _____

Bonus: On the back of the answer form, write a metaphor and a simile comparing the same two things.

©2002 by Evan-Moor Corp.

Name _____

Metaphors & Similes

Answer Form

Decide if the sentence on each task card is a metaphor or a simile. Write the card number under the correct heading.

Metaphors—figures of speech that make comparisons without using the words *like* or *as.*

Similes—figures of speech that make a comparison using the words *like* or *as.*

Metaphors   Similes

_____ _____ _____   _____ _____ _____

_____ _____ _____   _____ _____ _____

_____ _____ _____   _____ _____ _____

Bonus: On the back of the answer form, write a metaphor and a simile comparing the same two things.

©2002 by Evan-Moor Corp.

Metaphors & Similes

busy as a bee

1

Winter had come, like a quiet lullaby that lulled Autumn to sleep.

2

Tom ran down the field, untouched—a guided missile locked onto his target.

3

The lampposts stood like silent sentinels.

4

The runner was a thoroughbred, clearing the hurdles with ease.

5

Grandma's hat bloomed like a garden in early spring.

6

His words were hard and cold like the steel blade of a knife.

Metaphors & Similes

Metaphors & Similes

Metaphors & Similes

Metaphors & Similes

Metaphors & Similes

Metaphors & Similes

7

The wind from the open window blew the papers to the floor like fall leaves.

8

The trumpet's fanfare pierced the quiet like an arrow shot from an archer's bow.

9

The scarecrow stood alone, a former friend forgotten in the hustle of spring planting.

10

The roar of the car's engine was my morning alarm.

11

The green grass was a soft carpet for my bare toes.

12

The buds on a rose are like the promise of beauty in a symphony's opening notes.

Metaphors & Similes

Metaphors & Similes

Metaphors & Similes

Metaphors & Similes

Metaphors & Similes

Metaphors & Similes

Multiple-Meaning Words

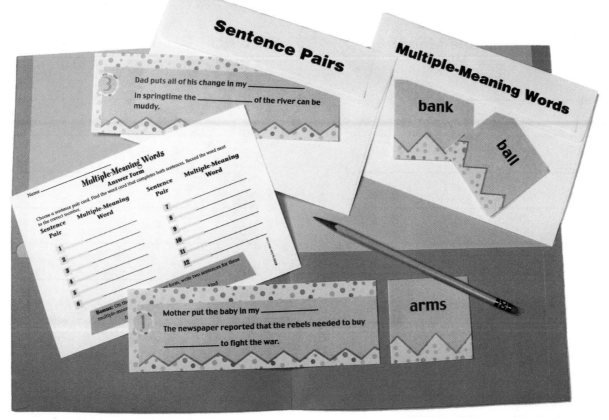

Preparing the Center

1. Prepare a folder following the directions on page 3. Laminate and cut out the cover design on page 97. Attach it to the front of the folder.

2. Laminate and cut out the sentence pair cards on pages 99–103. Place them in an envelope, label the envelope "Sentence Pairs," and put the envelope in the right-hand pocket of the folder. Laminate and cut out the word cards on page 105. Place them in an envelope, label the envelope "Multiple-Meaning Words," and put the envelope in the right-hand pocket.

3. Reproduce a supply of the answer form on page 96. Place copies in the left-hand pocket of the folder.

Using the Center

1. The student selects a sentence pair card and finds a word card that completes both sentences.

2. Then the student records the word on the answer form next to the number of the task card.

Name _____

Multiple-Meaning Words
Answer Form

Choose a sentence pair card. Find the word card that completes both sentences. Record the word next to the correct number.

Sentence Pair	Multiple-Meaning Word	Sentence Pair	Multiple-Meaning Word
1	_____	**7**	_____
2	_____	**8**	_____
3	_____	**9**	_____
4	_____	**10**	_____
5	_____	**11**	_____
6	_____	**12**	_____

Bonus: On the back of the answer form, write two sentences for these multiple-meaning words:

firm   yard   story   kind

©2002 by Evan-Moor Corp.

- -

Name _____

Multiple-Meaning Words
Answer Form

Choose a sentence pair card. Find the word card that completes both sentences. Record the word next to the correct number.

Sentence Pair	Multiple-Meaning Word	Sentence Pair	Multiple-Meaning Word
1	_____	**7**	_____
2	_____	**8**	_____
3	_____	**9**	_____
4	_____	**10**	_____
5	_____	**11**	_____
6	_____	**12**	_____

Bonus: On the back of the answer form, write two sentences for these multiple-meaning words:

firm   yard   story   kind

©2002 by Evan-Moor Corp.

Multiple Meanings

1

Mother put the baby in my _____.

The newspaper reported that the rebels needed to buy _____ to fight the war.

2

Paulo kicked the _____ through the uprights.

Cinderella wanted to go to the Prince's _____.

3

Dad puts all of his change in my _____.

In springtime the _____ of the river can be muddy.

4

The _____ of the tree is rough and bumpy.

My friend's dog Alf has a very loud _____.

Multiple-Meaning Words

Multiple-Meaning Words

Multiple-Meaning Words

Multiple-Meaning Words

5

The _____ made its home in a cool, dark cave.

The player swung her _____ and knocked the ball over the outfield fence.

6

The wind began to _____, so we moved the picnic indoors.

One _____ to the fragile shelf and all the dishes will fall.

7

The musician stores his horn in its _____.

Encyclopedia Brown solved the _____ of the missing letter.

8

I loved the pie-eating contest at the _____.

_____ play is essential to good sportsmanship.

Multiple-Meaning Words

Multiple-Meaning Words

Multiple-Meaning Words

Multiple-Meaning Words

9 When it's warm, Scott sleeps with the
_____ on.

Because he is a serious football _____, Steve
will be in the stands Friday night.

10 At camp I tanned the _____ of a rabbit.

Where will you _____ the present for your
mother?

11 The farmer keeps his animals in a _____.

I like to sign my name with Grandpa's _____.

12 I have to finish the _____ of the math
problems before lunch.

After running the race, he will need a _____.

Multiple-Meaning Words

Multiple-Meaning Words

Multiple-Meaning Words

Multiple-Meaning Words

rest	pen	hide
fan	fair	case
blow	bat	bark
bank	ball	arms

Multiple-Meaning Words

Multiple-Meaning Words

Multiple-Meaning Words

Multiple-Meaning Words

Multiple-Meaning Words

Multiple-Meaning Words

Multiple-Meaning Words

Multiple-Meaning Words

Multiple-Meaning Words

Multiple-Meaning Words

Multiple-Meaning Words

Multiple-Meaning Words

Persuasive Paragraphs

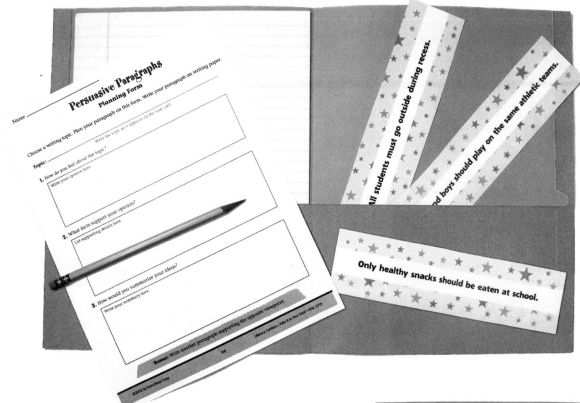

Preparing the Center

1. Prepare a folder following the directions on page 3. Laminate and cut out the cover design on page 109. Attach it to the front of the folder.

2. Laminate and cut out the task cards on pages 111 and 113. Place them in an envelope and put the envelope in the right-hand pocket of the folder.

3. Reproduce a supply of the planning form on page 108. Place copies and writing paper in the left-hand pocket of the folder.

Using the Center

1. The student chooses a writing topic and plans a paragraph using the planning form.

2. Then the student writes the paragraph on writing paper.

Persuasive Paragraphs
Planning Form

Choose a writing topic. Plan your paragraph on this form. Write your paragraph on writing paper.

Topic: _____

Write the topic as it appears on the task card.

1. How do you feel about the topic?

> Write your opinion here.

2. What facts support your opinion?

> List supporting details here.

3. How would you summarize your ideas?

> Write your summary here.

Bonus: Write another paragraph supporting the opposite viewpoint.

Persuasive Paragraphs

All students must go outside during recess.

Only healthy snacks should be eaten at school.

All skates should be prohibited on the playground.

Girls and boys should play on the same athletic teams.

All students should be required to do 30 minutes of homework each night.

Persuasive Paragraphs
Writing Topics

Persuasive Paragraphs
Writing Topics

Persuasive Paragraphs
Writing Topics

Persuasive Paragraphs
Writing Topics

Persuasive Paragraphs
Writing Topics

Fines should be collected for overdue library books.

Chocolate milk should be provided for all students.

Bus transportation should be provided for all students.

Students should attend school year-round.

Public libraries should be open 24 hours a day.

Persuasive Paragraphs
Writing Topics

Persuasive Paragraphs
Writing Topics

Persuasive Paragraphs
Writing Topics

Persuasive Paragraphs
Writing Topics

Persuasive Paragraphs
Writing Topics

Syllogisms

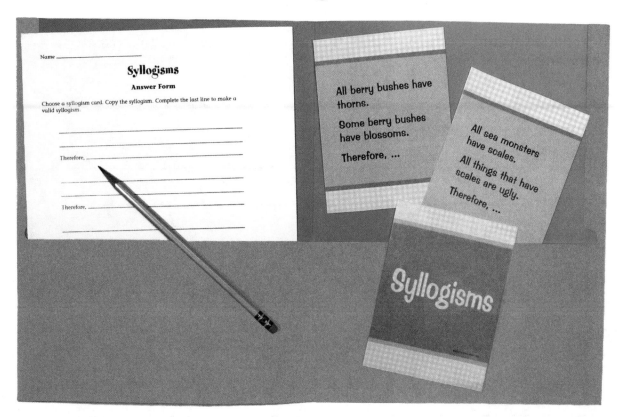

Preparing the Center

1. Prepare a folder following the directions on page 3. Laminate and cut out the cover design on page 117. Attach it to the front of the folder.

2. Laminate and cut out the task cards on pages 119–123. Place them in an envelope and put the envelope in the right-hand pocket of the folder.

3. Reproduce a supply of the answer form on page 116. Place copies in the left-hand pocket of the folder.

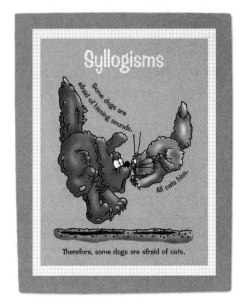

Using the Center

1. The student selects a task card and reads the syllogism. The last line of the syllogism is missing.

2. Then the student copies the syllogism on the answer form and writes a valid last line.

Syllogisms

Answer Form

Choose a syllogism card. Copy the syllogism. Complete the last line to make a valid syllogism.

_____

_____

Therefore, _____

_____

_____

Therefore, _____

_____

_____

Therefore, _____

_____

_____

Therefore, _____

Bonus: On the back of the answer form, write an original syllogism.

Syllogisms

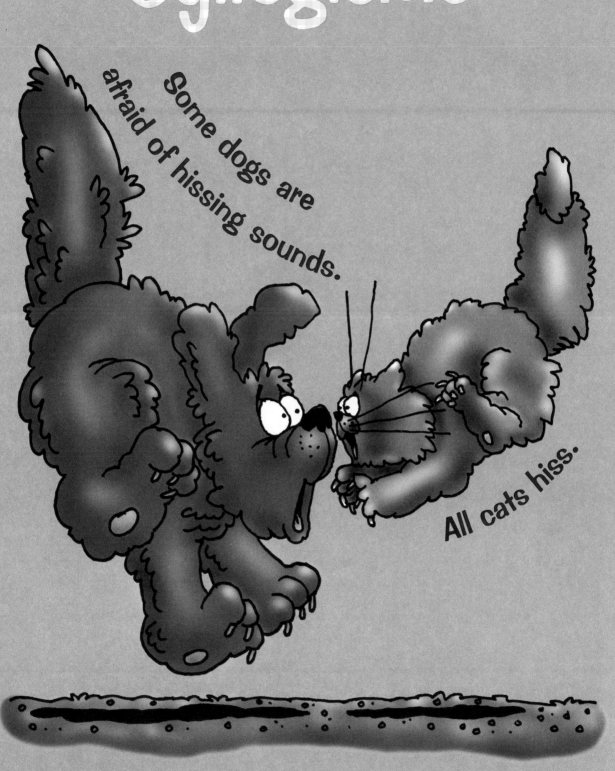

Some dogs are afraid of hissing sounds.

All cats hiss.

Therefore, some dogs are afraid of cats.

All sea monsters have scales.

All things that have scales are ugly.

Therefore,...

All roller coasters are exciting.

Some scary things are roller coasters.

Therefore,...

All candies are sweets.

Some sweets are chewy.

Therefore,...

All hornets are insects.

Some hornets are stinging creatures.

Therefore,...

Syllogisms Syllogisms

Syllogisms Syllogisms

All tables are furniture.

Some tables are made from wood.

Therefore,...

All people have teeth for chewing.

All children are people.

Therefore,...

All ladies like ice cream.

Some ladies are grandmas.

Therefore,...

All dogs are barking animals.

All German Shepherds are dogs.

Therefore,...

Syllogisms Syllogisms

Syllogisms Syllogisms

All birds have beaks.

Chickens are birds.

Therefore,...

All galaxies are out in space.

The Milky Way is a galaxy.

Therefore,...

All peaches are fruit.

No puppies are fruit.

Therefore,...

All athletes need good shoes.

All football players are athletes.

Therefore,...

Syllogisms Syllogisms

Syllogisms Syllogisms

Root Words

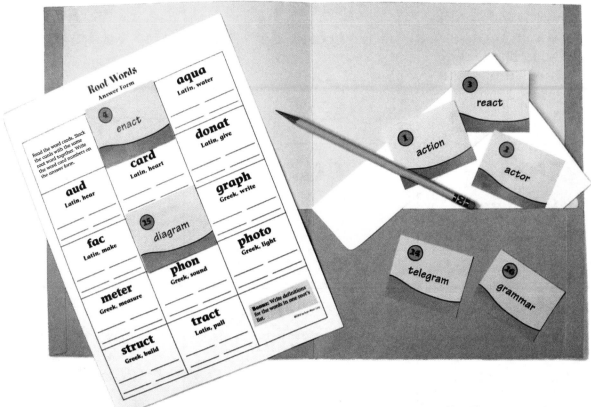

Preparing the Center

1. Prepare a folder following the directions on page 3. Laminate and cut out the cover design on page 127. Attach it to the front of the folder.

2. Laminate and cut out the task cards on pages 129–133. Place them in an envelope and put the envelope in the right-hand pocket of the folder.

3. Reproduce a supply of the answer form on page 126. Place copies in the left-hand pocket of the folder.

Using the Center

1. The student stacks word cards with a common root together.

2. Then the student writes the numbers of the cards on the answer form.

Root Words

Answer Form

Read the word cards. Stack the cards with the same root word together. Write the word card numbers on the answer form.	**act** Latin, do _____ _____ _____ _____	**aqua** Latin, water _____ _____ _____ _____
aud Latin, hear _____ _____	**card** Latin, heart _____ _____	**donat** Latin, give _____ _____
fac Latin, make _____ _____	**gram** Greek, letter _____ _____	**graph** Greek, write _____ _____
meter Greek, measure _____ _____ _____ _____	**phon** Greek, sound _____ _____ _____ _____	**photo** Greek, light _____ _____ _____ _____
struct Greek, build _____ _____ _____ _____	**tract** Latin, pull _____ _____	**Bonus:** Write definitions for the words in one root's list.

Root Words

1 action

2 actor

3 react

4 enact

5 aquarium

6 aquatic

7 aquamarine

8 audience

9 auditorium

10 audition

11 audible

12 cardiac

13 cardiology

14 cardiovascular

15 donation

16 attract

Root Words

©2002 by Evan-Moor Corp.

Root Words

©2002 by Evan-Moor Corp.

Root Words

©2002 by Evan-Moor Corp.

Root Words

©2002 by Evan-Moor Corp.

Root Words

©2002 by Evan-Moor Corp.

Root Words

©2002 by Evan-Moor Corp.

Root Words

©2002 by Evan-Moor Corp.

Root Words

©2002 by Evan-Moor Corp.

Root Words

©2002 by Evan-Moor Corp.

Root Words

©2002 by Evan-Moor Corp.

Root Words

©2002 by Evan-Moor Corp.

Root Words

©2002 by Evan-Moor Corp.

Root Words

©2002 by Evan-Moor Corp.

Root Words

©2002 by Evan-Moor Corp.

Root Words

©2002 by Evan-Moor Corp.

Root Words

©2002 by Evan-Moor Corp.

17 donor	**21** manufacture	**25** diagram	**29** biography
18 pardon	**22** benefactor	**26** grammar	**30** thermometer
19 donate	**23** facsimile	**27** photograph	**31** centimeter
20 factory	**24** telegram	**28** autograph	**32** traction

Root Words ©2002 by Evan-Moor Corp.

Root Words ©2002 by Evan-Moor Corp.

Root Words ©2002 by Evan-Moor Corp.

Root Words ©2002 by Evan-Moor Corp.

Root Words ©2002 by Evan-Moor Corp.

Root Words ©2002 by Evan-Moor Corp.

Root Words ©2002 by Evan-Moor Corp.

Root Words ©2002 by Evan-Moor Corp.

Root Words ©2002 by Evan-Moor Corp.

Root Words ©2002 by Evan-Moor Corp.

Root Words ©2002 by Evan-Moor Corp.

Root Words ©2002 by Evan-Moor Corp.

Root Words ©2002 by Evan-Moor Corp.

Root Words ©2002 by Evan-Moor Corp.

Root Words ©2002 by Evan-Moor Corp.

Root Words ©2002 by Evan-Moor Corp.

(33) diameter	(37) microphone	(41) photosynthesis	(45) instruct
(34) barometer	(38) phonics	(42) photogenic	(46) destruction
(35) symphony	(39) photograph	(43) structure	(47) tractor
(36) telephone	(40) telephoto	(44) construct	(48) extract

Root Words ©2002 by Evan-Moor Corp.

Root Words ©2002 by Evan-Moor Corp.

Root Words ©2002 by Evan-Moor Corp.

Root Words ©2002 by Evan-Moor Corp.

Root Words ©2002 by Evan-Moor Corp.

Root Words ©2002 by Evan-Moor Corp.

Root Words ©2002 by Evan-Moor Corp.

Root Words ©2002 by Evan-Moor Corp.

Root Words ©2002 by Evan-Moor Corp.

Root Words ©2002 by Evan-Moor Corp.

Root Words ©2002 by Evan-Moor Corp.

Root Words ©2002 by Evan-Moor Corp.

Root Words ©2002 by Evan-Moor Corp.

Root Words ©2002 by Evan-Moor Corp.

Root Words ©2002 by Evan-Moor Corp.

Root Words ©2002 by Evan-Moor Corp.

Using Commas

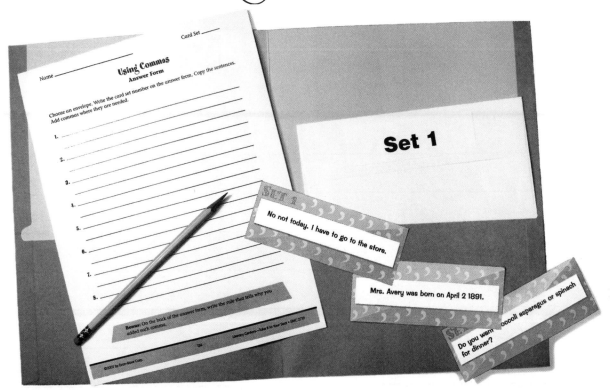

Preparing the Center

1. Prepare a folder following the directions on page 3. Laminate and cut out the cover design on page 137. Attach it to the front of the folder.

2. Laminate and cut out the task cards on pages 139–143. Place each set in an envelope, label the envelope, and put the envelopes in the right-hand pocket of the folder.

3. Reproduce a supply of the answer form on page 136. Place copies in the left-hand pocket of the folder.

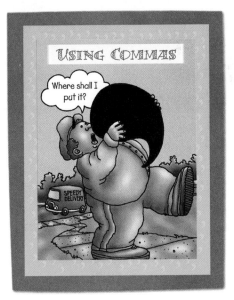

Using the Center

1. The student selects a task card and reads the sentence.

2. Then the student copies the sentence on the answer form, adding commas appropriately. **Note:** Make additional task card sets if your students are ready for more advanced comma usage.

3. The student repeats these steps for the remaining sentences in the set.

Using Commas
Answer Form

Choose an envelope. Write the card set number on the answer form. Copy the sentences. Add commas where they are needed.

1. _____

_____

2. _____

_____

3. _____

_____

4. _____

_____

5. _____

_____

6. _____

_____

7. _____

_____

8. _____

_____

Bonus: On the back of the answer form, write the rule that tells why you added each comma.

USING COMMAS

Well will you come to the party?

I went to the soccer game with Leo Mary and Paul.

Dave planted the tomatoes carrots and lettuce.

On the trip we had a flat tire Amy was carsick and then we got lost.

Frankie will you help me feed the dog?

No not today. I have to go to the store.

I can help you after supper Sara if that's not too late.

Okay Sara I'll see you when you get back.

USING COMMAS

USING COMMAS

USING COMMAS

USING COMMAS

USING COMMAS

USING COMMAS

USING COMMAS

USING COMMAS

Yes my mother said I could.

Anthony where were you?

I have to set the table start the barbecue and make the salad.

Snickers Blossom and Gramps are friendly puppies.

Mrs. Avery was born on April 2 1891.

Someday I want to go to London England.

Hurry up Peter if you're coming with me.

No you can't go this time.

USING COMMAS ©2002 by Evan-Moor Corp.

USING COMMAS ©2002 by Evan-Moor Corp.

USING COMMAS ©2002 by Evan-Moor Corp.

USING COMMAS ©2002 by Evan-Moor Corp.

USING COMMAS ©2002 by Evan-Moor Corp.

USING COMMAS ©2002 by Evan-Moor Corp.

USING COMMAS ©2002 by Evan-Moor Corp.

USING COMMAS ©2002 by Evan-Moor Corp.

SET 3

Yes I would like to have your old coat.

SET 3

I think this is your lunch Fernando.

SET 3

Do you want broccoli asparagus or spinach for dinner?

SET 3

I can see Debbie that you are getting ready.

SET 3

My bag was filled with books papers pencils and gum.

SET 3

Gary will you please get started now.

SET 3

Pop drove his pickup truck all the way to pueblo Colorado.

SET 3

Jack climbed the beanstalk knocked on the giant's door and asked for bread.

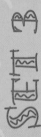

USING COMMAS

©2002 by Evan-Moor Corp.

USING COMMAS

©2002 by Evan-Moor Corp.

USING COMMAS

©2002 by Evan-Moor Corp.

USING COMMAS

©2002 by Evan-Moor Corp.

USING COMMAS

©2002 by Evan-Moor Corp.

USING COMMAS

©2002 by Evan-Moor Corp.

USING COMMAS

©2002 by Evan-Moor Corp.

USING COMMAS

©2002 by Evan-Moor Corp.

Write a Story

Preparing the Center

1. Prepare a folder following the directions on page 3. Laminate and cut out the cover design on page 147. Attach it to the front of the folder.

2. Laminate and cut out the task cards on pages 149–153. Place them in an envelope and put the envelope in the right-hand pocket of the folder.

3. Reproduce a supply of the writing form on page 146. Place copies in the left-hand pocket of the folder.

Using the Center

1. The student selects a story starter from the task cards.

2. Then the student writes a story.

Write a Story
Writing Form

Choose a story starter card. Write a story.

_____

_____

_____

_____

_____

_____

_____

_____

_____

_____

_____

_____

_____

_____

_____

Bonus: Illustrate the story.

Write a Story

When I looked out my window this morning,
I saw strange footprints in the snow.

Tom and I were putting the finishing touches on
our snowperson, when a strange voice said...

Suppose you live where there is no snow.
Think of a creative way to make a "snowman"
using something in your environment.

Imagine the playground was covered with snow
that wouldn't melt.

Write a Story

Write a Story

Write a Story

Write a Story

Frederick was having fun sliding around on the snow. Then he came to the top of the hill.

What would it be like to be a snowflake? Where would you land? How would it feel to float through the sky?

The blizzard had been raging for a week. The TV didn't work, and I was sick of the video games. Suddenly I had a great idea. I would...

Shoveling snow is a thing of the past! I have discovered a new way to clear my driveway.

Write a Story

Write a Story

Write a Story

Write a Story

When I pushed the back door open, snow burst into the kitchen. It was cold, wet, and purple!

Blizzard Basin schools have had 61 snow days this year. Superintendent Flake has proposed a creative plan to make up the time.

The school bus is stuck in a giant snowdrift. The radio is out. You have a plan for keeping warm.

There's a mysterious message written in the snow in front of the school. Who wrote it? What does it say?

Write a Story

©2002 by Evan-Moor Corp.

Write a Story

©2002 by Evan-Moor Corp.

Write a Story

©2002 by Evan-Moor Corp.

Write a Story

©2002 by Evan-Moor Corp.

Homophones

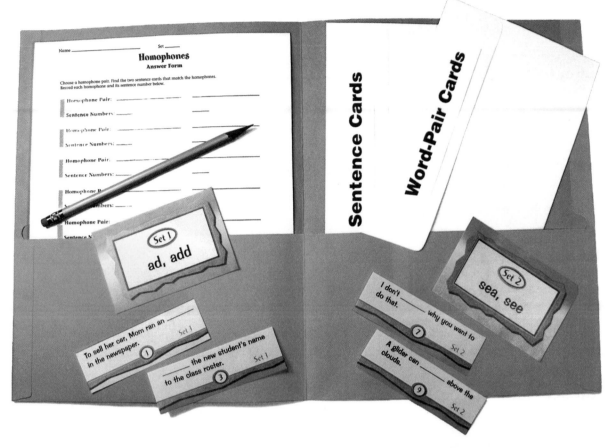

Preparing the Center

1. Prepare a folder following the directions on page 3. Laminate and cut out the cover design on page 157. Attach it to the front of the folder.

2. Laminate and cut out the task cards on pages 159–165. Place the word-pair cards and the sentence cards from each set in separate envelopes, label the envelopes, and put the envelopes in the right-hand pocket of the folder.

3. Reproduce a supply of the answer form on page 156. Place copies in the left-hand pocket of the folder.

Using the Center

1. The student matches homophone pairs with the sentences in which they fit.

2. Then the student records the sentence numbers on the answer form.

Homophones
Answer Form

Choose a homophone pair. Find the two sentence cards that match the homophones.
Record each homophone and its sentence number below.

Homophone Pair: _____   _____

Sentence Numbers: _____   _____

Homophone Pair: _____   _____

Sentence Numbers: _____   _____

Homophone Pair: _____   _____

Sentence Numbers: _____   _____

Homophone Pair: _____   _____

Sentence Numbers: _____   _____

Homophone Pair: _____   _____

Sentence Numbers: _____   _____

Homophone Pair: _____   _____

Sentence Numbers: _____   _____

Homophone Pair: _____   _____

Sentence Numbers: _____   _____

Bonus: On the back of the answer form, write sentences for these
sets of three homophones:

sent, cent, scent	so, sew, sow
pair, pare, pear	where, wear, ware

Homophones

night   knight

Set 1

ad, add

Set 1

ant, aunt

Set 1

ate, eight

Set 1

bail, bale

Set 1

brake, break

Set 1

coarse, course

Set 1

flour, flower

Set 1

missed, mist

Homophones

Homophones

Homophones

Homophones

Homophones

Homophones

Homophones

Homophones

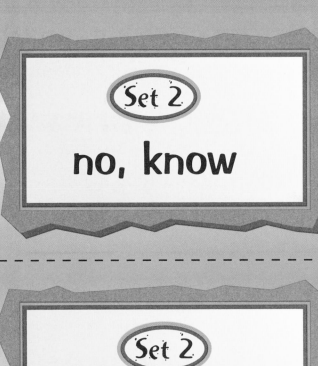
Set 2

no, know

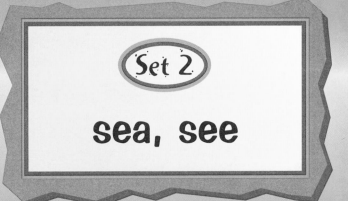
Set 2

sea, see

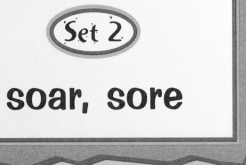
Set 2

soar, sore

Set 2

stairs, stares

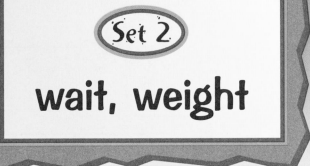
Set 2

wait, weight

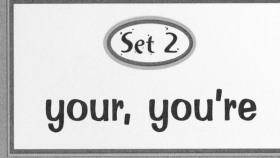
Set 2

your, you're

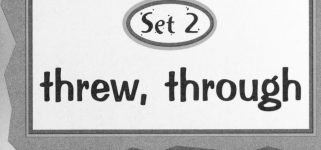
Set 2

threw, through

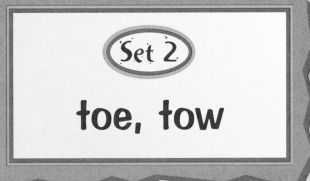
Set 2

toe, tow

Homophones

Homophones

Homophones

Homophones

Homophones

Homophones

Homophones

Homophones

To sell her car, Mom ran an _____ in the newspaper.

1
Set 1

Just press on the _____ to make the car stop.

2
Set 1

_____ the new student's name to the class roster.

3
Set 1

The vase will _____ if you knock it off the shelf.

4
Set 1

The only uninvited guest at the picnic was a nasty red _____.

5
Set 1

The sandpaper is so _____, it smoothes the wood quickly.

6
Set 1

My favorite _____ loves to talk on the phone.

7
Set 1

Mr. Smith teaches a _____ in biology.

8
Set 1

Popeye _____ spinach whenever he got into a jam.

9
Set 1

Mrs. Black measured the _____ for the biscuits.

10
Set 1

An octopus has _____ arms.

11
Set 1

Penny wore a _____ in her hair for the dance.

12
Set 1

She had to _____ the water out of the bottom of the boat.

13
Set 1

Everyone _____ the same question on the quiz.

14
Set 1

My horses whinny when they see me arrive with a new _____ of hay.

15
Set 1

The attachment on the hose makes a gentle _____.

16
Set 1

Homophone Sentences

Homophone Sentences

©2002 by Evan-Moor Corp.

Homophone Sentences

©2002 by Evan-Moor Corp.

Homophone Sentences

©2002 by Evan-Moor Corp.

Homophone Sentences

©2002 by Evan-Moor Corp.

Homophone Sentences

©2002 by Evan-Moor Corp.

Homophone Sentences

©2002 by Evan-Moor Corp.

Homophone Sentences

©2002 by Evan-Moor Corp.

Homophone Sentences

©2002 by Evan-Moor Corp.

Homophone Sentences

©2002 by Evan-Moor Corp.

Homophone Sentences

©2002 by Evan-Moor Corp.

Homophone Sentences

©2002 by Evan-Moor Corp.

Homophone Sentences

©2002 by Evan-Moor Corp.

Homophone Sentences

©2002 by Evan-Moor Corp.

Homophone Sentences

©2002 by Evan-Moor Corp.

Homophone Sentences

©2002 by Evan-Moor Corp.

A perfect paper means you made _____ mistakes.

① Set 2

We have to _____ until the cookies come out of the oven.

② Set 2

Do you _____ whether Sammy will be at the game.

③ Set 2

We recorded the _____ of each rock in the collection.

④ Set 2

The Pilgrims sailed across the _____.

⑤ Set 2

_____ kitten is the cutest one in the neighborhood.

⑥ Set 2

I don't _____ why you want to do that.

⑦ Set 2

If _____ sure you will be there, I will call in a reservation.

⑧ Set 2

A glider can _____ above the clouds.

⑨ Set 2

He _____ the trash into the recycling bin.

⑩ Set 2

He can't play in the match because he has a _____ foot.

⑪ Set 2

The mouse ran _____ the maze in record time.

⑫ Set 2

If I stand on the _____ I can see out the high window.

⑬ Set 2

He stubbed his _____ on the ladder.

⑭

The man at the garage _____ at the gauges as he tests the car.

⑮ Set 2

His van can _____ the boat to the lake.

⑯ Set 2

Homophone Sentences

Homophone Sentences

Homophone Sentences

Homophone Sentences

Homophone Sentences

Homophone Sentences

Homophone Sentences

Homophone Sentences

Homophone Sentences

Homophone Sentences

Homophone Sentences

Homophone Sentences

Homophone Sentences

Homophone Sentences

Homophone Sentences

Homophone Sentences

Poetry

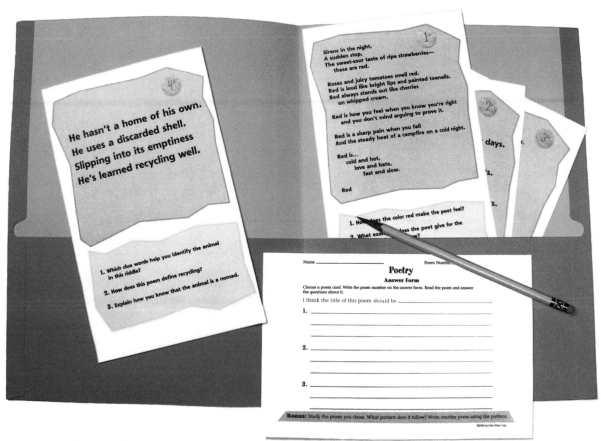

He hasn't a home of his own.
He uses a discarded shell.
Slipping into its emptiness
He's learned recycling well.

1. Which clue words help you identify the animal in this riddle?

2. How does this poem define recycling?

3. Explain how you know that the animal is a nomad.

Sirens in the night.
A sudden stop.
The sweet-sour taste of ripe strawberries—
these are red.

Roses and juicy tomatoes smell red.
Red is loud like bright lips and painted toenails.
Red always stands out like cherries
on whipped cream.

Red is how you feel when you know you're right
and you don't mind arguing to prove it.

Red is a sharp pain when you fall
And the steady heat of a campfire on a cold night.

Red is...
cold and hot,
love and hate,
fast and slow.

Red

Name _____ Poem Number _____

Poetry
Answer Form
Choose a poem card. Write the poem number on the answer form. Read the poem and answer the questions about it.

I think the title of this poem should be _____

1. _____
   _____
   _____

2. _____
   _____
   _____

3. _____
   _____

Bonus: Study the poem you chose. What pattern does it follow? Write another poem using the pattern.

Preparing the Center

1. Prepare a folder following the directions on page 3. Laminate and cut out the cover design on page 169. Attach it to the front of the folder.

2. Laminate and cut out the task cards on pages 171–177. Place them in an envelope and put the envelope in the right-hand pocket of the folder.

3. Reproduce a supply of the answer form on page 168. Place copies in the left-hand pocket of the folder.

Using the Center

1. The student selects and reads a poem card.

2. Then the student answers the questions about the poem.

If it flows on your tongue like candy and into your ear like music...it's poetry.
Greg Denman

Name _____ Poem Number _____

Poetry

Answer Form

Choose a poem card. Write the poem number on the answer form. Read the poem and answer the questions about it.

I think the title of this poem should be _____

1. _____

_____

2. _____

_____

3. _____

_____

Bonus: Study the poem you chose. What pattern does it follow? Write another poem using the pattern.

Name _____ Poem Number _____

Poetry

Answer Form

Choose a poem card. Write the poem number on the answer form. Read the poem and answer the questions about it.

I think the title of this poem should be _____

1. _____

_____

2. _____

_____

3. _____

_____

Bonus: Study the poem you chose. What pattern does it follow? Write another poem using the pattern.

1

Sirens in the night,
A sudden stop,
The sweet-sour taste of ripe strawberries—
these are red.

Roses and juicy tomatoes smell red.
Red is loud like bright lips and painted toenails.
Red always stands out like cherries
on whipped cream.

Red is how you feel when you know you're right
and you don't mind arguing to prove it.

Red is a sharp pain when you fall
And the steady heat of a campfire on a cold night.

Red is...
    cold and hot,
    love and hate,
        fast and slow.

Red

1. How does the color red make the poet feel?

2. What examples does the poet give for the opposites fast and slow?

3. What opposites can you think of to support love and hate?

2

Gather colors.
Gather sounds.
Store them safe for gray days.
Gather smells.
Gather tastes.
They will be your bouquets.
Gather smiles.
Gather hugs.
They will warm the cold days.
Gather memories.
Gather friends.
They'll be with you always.

1. What is the theme of this poem?

2. Which word best describes the poet?
    materialistic   sentimental   literal

3. What does the phrase "your bouquets" symbolize?

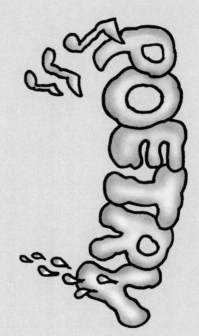

This is my crayon box.
Listen as it talks.
   Red shouts.
   Green sings.
   Yellow laughs.
   Gray whispers.
   Black demands.
   White apologizes.
   Pink giggles.
   Blue sighs softly.
This is my crayon box.
Listen as it talks.

1. How would the color brown say something?

2. What comparison underlies this whole poem?

3. Each color in the crayon box has a personality.
Write several words to describe the personality
of each of these colors:

   red   white   gray   black

4

He hasn't a home of his own.

He uses a discarded shell.

Slipping into its emptiness

He's learned recycling well.

1. Which clue words help you identify the animal
in this riddle?

2. How does this poem define recycling?

3. Explain how you know that the animal is a nomad.

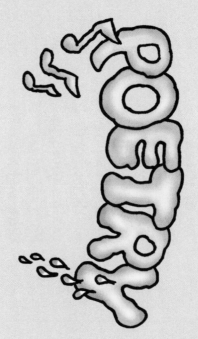

5

Ivory bonnets alive with the wind

Swagger above a carpet of lavish moss.

The wind is sweet and tastes of summer.

---

1. What are the ivory bonnets in this poem?

2. Does this poem describe a desert scene or a forest scene? Tell why you answered as you did.

3. Sometimes poets use their senses in unexpected ways. What unexpected use of a sense can you find in this poem?

6

Some leaves and stuff fell on

A layer of sand.

Next more sand covered the leaves. The layers got

Deeper and deeper.

Slowly many years passed—

Time is an important ingredient in the process.

Over and over the layers formed and settled.

New layers pressed down on the first ones.

Eventually the layers become rock.

---

1. What process does this poem describe?

2. What ingredients of the process are listed in the poem?

3. This poem is called an acrostic.   Lovely

   Here is another simple acrostic.   Even

                                             After

                                             Falling

   What is the main attribute of an acrostic poem?

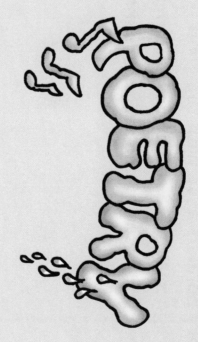

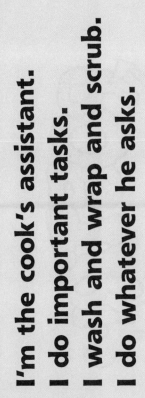

7

I'm the cook's assistant.
I do important tasks.
I wash and wrap and scrub.
I do whatever he asks.

I'm the cook's assistant.
I butter and I beat.
I pour and shake and stir.
And then, of course, I eat!

1. Does the poet enjoy being the cook's assistant?
   How do you know?

2. What nine specific tasks does the poet complete?

3. This poem was written about a small child
   helping in the kitchen. Write several adjectives
   that describe how the child feels.

8

Three sisters dressed all in green—
Tall Sister Corn, twisting Sister Bean,
Sister Squash wound 'round their feet—
The better they grow, the more we eat.

1. This simple verse tells about the three
   sisters of traditional Native American
   tales. Who are the three sisters?

2. What do you know about the Native
   American who might have written
   this verse?

3. What do you know about the
   way in which the three different
   vegetables grow?

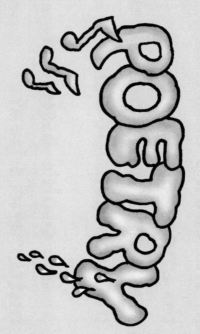

Idioms

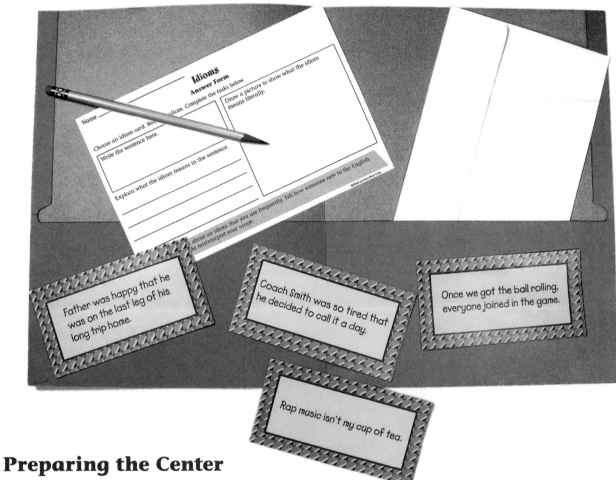

Idioms
Answer Form

Name _____

Choose an idiom card. Re____ _idiom. Complete the tasks below.

Write the sentence here.

Draw a picture to show what the idiom means literally.

Explain what the idiom means in the sentence.

_____ about an idiom that you use frequently. Tell how someone new to the English _____ght misinterpret your usage.

Father was happy that he was on the last leg of his long trip home.

Coach Smith was so tired that he decided to call it a day.

Once we got the ball rolling, everyone joined in the game.

Rap music isn't my cup of tea.

Preparing the Center

1. Prepare a folder following the directions on page 3. Laminate and cut out the cover design on page 181. Attach it to the front of the folder.

2. Laminate and cut out the task cards on pages 183–188. Place them in an envelope and put the envelope in the right-hand pocket of the folder.

3. Reproduce a supply of the answer form on page 180. Place copies in the left-hand pocket of the folder.

Using the Center

1. The student selects a task card and reads the sentence containing an idiom.

2. On the answer form, the student writes what the idiom means in the sentence and draws a picture of the literal meaning.

Name _____

Idioms
Answer Form

Choose an idiom card. Read the idiom. Complete the tasks below.

Write the sentence here.	Draw a picture to show what the idiom means literally.

Explain what the idiom means in the sentence.

_____

_____

_____

_____

Bonus: Write about an idiom that you use frequently. Tell how someone new to the English language might misinterpret your usage.

©2002 by Evan-Moor Corp.

- -

Name _____

Idioms
Answer Form

Choose an idiom card. Read the idiom. Complete the tasks below.

Write the sentence here.	Draw a picture to show what the idiom means literally.

Explain what the idiom means in the sentence.

_____

_____

_____

_____

Bonus: Write about an idiom that you use frequently. Tell how someone new to the English language might misinterpret your usage.

©2002 by Evan-Moor Corp.

Idioms

He eats like a bird.

He eats like a horse.

Father was happy that he was on the last leg of his long trip home.

Rap music isn't my cup of tea.

Coach Smith was so tired that he decided to call it a day.

You can tell by her successful garden that she has a green thumb.

Once we got the ball rolling, everyone joined in the game.

Drop me a line when you get to camp.

Idioms

Idioms

Idioms

Idioms

Idioms

Idioms

Bruce got cold feet just before his entrance in the first act.

My brother's new car hugged the road as it took the curve.

The tap dancer stole the spotlight.

Scott was down in the dumps after losing his notebook.

Becky was so grouchy that I knew she had gotten up on the wrong side of the bed.

We finished our assignment, so we sat around shooting the breeze.

Idioms

Idioms

Idioms

Idioms

Idioms

Idioms

I can't go to the movies tonight, but I'll take a rain check.

The fact that I forgot to ask for a receipt is really eating at me.

Mrs. Ramirez thought I had lost the book, so I set her straight.

I have to get up early, so it's time to hit the hay.

Learning to play the new video game was a piece of cake.

If we want to win the game, we all need to stick together.

Idioms

Idioms

Idioms

Idioms

Idioms

Idioms

Answer Key

Page 4—Antonyms

Blue Cards
absent	present
achieve	fail
advance	retreat
affirm	deny
admire	detest
attack	defend
awkward	graceful
annoy	soothe
bent	straight

Pink Cards
brave	cowardly
blunt	sharp
capture	release
cheap	expensive
cruel	kind
destroy	create
expand	shrink
forgive	blame
fresh	stale

Green Cards
idle	active
innocent	guilty
level	uneven
obvious	hidden
plentiful	sparse
positive	negative
praise	criticism
prohibit	allow
ridiculous	sensible

Purple Cards
sharp	dull
thorough	incomplete
unique	common
vanish	appear
rapid	slow
stiff	flexible
suspect	trust
temporary	permanent
triumph	defeat

Page 17—Alphabetical Order

Set 1
acid
chase
environment
fiction
machine
omnivorous
revise
speculate

Set 2
morning
mortar
owner
package
plaster
quote
racket
reason

Set 3
sanitary
sarcastic
satire
satisfy
sausage
save
science
scissors

Set 4
grief
grind
groggy
groom
grouch
ground
group
grove

Set 5
hyacinth
hydraulic
hydrogen
hyena
hygiene
hyperactive
hypnotic
hypothesis

Set 6
radar
radial
radiant
radiate
radiator
radical
radio
radioactive

Page 27—Parts of Speech

Set 1
Noun—heap
Verbs—sleep, perch
Adjectives—different, comfortable
Adverb—upside down

Set 2
Nouns—pieces, mouth
Verb—give
Adjectives—your, three
Adverb—too

Set 3
Nouns—stickers, people
Verb—move
Adjectives—wing-like, new
Adverb—many

Page 37—Synonyms
capable	competent
achieve	accomplish
question	interrogate
astonish	surprise
start	initiate
border	edge
brave	courageous
calm	serene
decrease	lessen
danger	peril
disaster	catastrophe
finish	complete
own	possess
beginner	novice
praise	applaud
supply	furnish

Page 49—Combining Sentences

Sentences may be combined correctly in several different ways.

Page 59—Analogies

A stethoscope is to a doctor as a paintbrush is to an artist.

A tablecloth is to a table as a scarf is to a head.

Heavy is to light as speedy is to pokey.

A puppy is to a dog as a cub is to a bear.

Film is to a camera as ink is to a pen.

A hamster is to a running wheel as a runner is to a track.

Gas is to tank as salt is to shaker.

Suspenders are to pants as trellises are to vines.

Model T is to automobile as Pony Express is to mail service.

A flute is to a piccolo as a moving van is to a pickup truck.

Three is to nine as ten is to one hundred.

Fast is to rapid as still is to calm.

Page 69—Kinds of Sentences

Declarative Sentences
2. Many candies are made out of chocolate.
3. Carob is a substitute for chocolate.
5. Italian children like to eat chewy nougats.
7. Add two numbers to get a sum.
8. Mathematics is the science of numbers.
11. You divide to find the quotient.
14. Rock climbing is a strenuous sport.
16. When the guide yells, "Belay!" I respond, "Belay on."
17. Hiking is not the same as rock climbing.

Interrogative Sentences
1. Do you have a sweet tooth?
6. Have you ever made fudge?
10. Is the stop sign an octagon or a pentagon?
15. Can you rappel down the side of a mountain?
18. Do you have climbing shoes?

Exclamatory Sentences
4. Absolutely no candy for you!
9. I love all kinds of math!
12. I can't believe I got the answer!
13. Help, I'm losing my grip!

Page 79—Main Ideas & Supporting Details

Paragraph 1
Rhinos are strange-looking.

- wrinkled nose with two vertical horns
- short, clumsy legs seem too small
- thick, rough skin hangs in folds

Paragraph 2
Water moves from liquid form to water vapor and back to liquid form over and over again.

- when it is heated, water changes from a liquid form into gas
- when water vapor is cooled, it turns back into tiny droplets

Paragraph 3
A puppet can be a famous star.

- Charlie McCarthy was a wooden dummy.
- Charlie traveled around the world with Edgar Bergen, the ventriloquist.
- Charlie was so popular that he got more mail than Mr. Bergen.

Paragraph 4
The beaver is well-suited to its environment.

- broad tail for steering as it swims
- webbed back feet help it swim
- strong front paws help it dig and carry
- large orange front teeth for gnawing

Paragraph 5
George Washington was important to the development of modern farming.

- studied the best way to plant and harvest crops
- experimented with new farming equipment
- built a 16-sided barn for threshing
- kept meticulous records about crops and their yields

Paragraph 6
The Nile is one of the birthplaces of modern civilization.

- water from the river made a good place for ancient peoples to live
- fertile soil made a good place for people to farm

Paragraph 7
Whales can be identified by their blows.

- Blue whale has a narrow, high blow.
- Right whale makes two low blows from twin blowholes.
- Humpback whale has a low blow.
- Sperm whale makes a blow that is angled forward and to the left.